CROSS-STITCH

Simple-to-Sew

CROSS-STITCH

*Master new sewing skills with these
simple-to-make projects*

DOROTHEA HALL

B T Batsford Limited, London

First published in Great Britain by B. T. Batsford Ltd.
4 Fitzhardinge Street, London W1H 0AH

ISBN 0-7134-7928-0

A catalogue record for this book is available from
the British Library

This book was designed and produced by
Quintet Publishing plc.
The Old Brewery
6 Blundell Street
London N7 9BH

Creative Director: Richard Dewing
Designer: Isobel Gillan
Project Editor: Anna Briffa
Editor: Samantha Gray
Illustrator: Nicola Gregory
Chart Illustrator: Jennie Dooge
Photographer: Andrew Sydenham

Typeset in Great Britain by
Central Southern Typesetters, Eastbourne
Manufactured in Singapore by Eray Scan Pte. Ltd.
Printed in Singapore by Star Standard Industries Pte. Ltd.

ACKNOWLEDGEMENTS
The Publishers would like to thank the following
for their help and advice on this title:
The Quilt Room, 20 West Street, Dorking, Surrey,
and Creativity, Needlecraft Specialists,
45 New Oxford Street, London.

CONTENTS

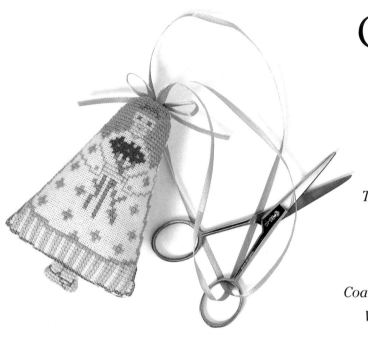

INTRODUCTION

Cross-stitch embroidery is an immensely satisfying and rewarding craft, offering tremendous scope for making beautiful gifts and adding to your own personal skills. The book contains a broad selection of practical projects to suit all tastes and occasions – each one carefully chosen for the simple skills involved in making it. Indeed, some projects, such as the jampot covers, paperweights and greetings cards, are "made up" without any additional sewing. The bookmark, for example, is so easy to complete that even a beginner to cross-stitch and general sewing could make it in an evening!

Once you have a little practice in cross-stitch, you may like to "mix and match" the motifs, for instance, working the wild flowers of the paperweights for greetings cards and so on.

You may also like to further personalize your embroidery with names, dates or dedications using the alphabets given on pages 45–48. The permutations are endless! Use this collection of ideas to create something special and make your cross-stitch quite unique.

BASIC MATERIALS

Fabrics

For best results, cross-stitch embroidery is worked on an evenweave fabric – this is any fabric that has the same number of threads counted in both directions, usually over 1in/2.5cm, and are generally referred to as 12, 14, 18 count or gauge, for example. The evenness of the weave ensures that all the cross-stitches are consistently square.

Linen is the traditional fabric for cross-stitching and is available in a good range of counts and colours. Natural colours are traditional and always popular and the slightly uneven appearance of many linens gives it a charming hand-woven look.

Evenweave cottons and cotton/linen mixes are also available in a great variety of colours and counts. Many of these examples can be bought as small sizes in handy packs, which is more economical than buying from the roll if you want to make only a single item. Evenweave cottons may feel very stiff due to the dressing they are given by the manufacturers. Although this can be washed out before you embroider to give a softer fabric, working on stiffened fabric may help you to stitch with an even tension.

Threads

Embroidery threads: almost any type of embroidery thread can be used for cross-stitch embroidery, depending on the fabric count and thickness of thread. For the purposes of this book, DMC stranded embroidery cotton has been used throughout. Generally speaking, fewer strands are used on finer fabric and for suggesting fine detail, and vice versa. The exact number of strands used for the projects in the book is given with the individual instructions.

Tacking thread is a soft, loosely twisted cotton. The main advantages in using it are that (unlike ordinary sewing thread) it does not leave marks when pressed with an iron; should it get tangled it will break rather than damage the fabric, and it is more economical than sewing thread.

Sewing threads are fine, tightly twisted and strong. They are made in an excellent range of colours from cotton or cotton/polyester mixes.

Needles

Tapestry needles: for working cross-stitch on evenweave fabrics, round-ended tapestry needles are used. Their smooth tips enable the needle to pass easily through the fabric without piercing the threads, available in sizes 18–26.

Crewel needles: for additional embroidery, such as the open buttonhole stitch on the shoe bag, page 11, medium-sized crewel needles are used. These have sharp points and long oval eyes and are available in sizes 1–10.

Sharp sewing needles: a selection will be needed for making up the projects.

Hoop

Although many people prefer to work small amounts of cross-stitch in the hand, there are advantages to using a hoop. With the fabric evenly stretched, it helps to maintain an even tension to the cross-stitch. When the hoop is supported, it leaves both hands free to stitch – with one hand on top and the other below. It is possible to stitch evenly and faster this way.

Sewing machine

A sewing machine is useful for making-up purposes, especially for bigger projects where longer seams are involved. In such cases, a machine-sewn seam is not only stronger than a hand-sewn one, but also quicker to complete.

General accessories

You will also need the following items: stainless steel pins, a fabric tape measure, a thimble for hand sewing, especially through bulky seams, a ruler and pencil, and ideally three types of scissors: a pair of sharp dressmaker's shears for cutting out fabric, small embroidery scissors for snipping into seam allowances and trimming threads, and general purpose scissors for cutting paper, cords and so on; an iron and ironing board – preferably a thermostatically controlled iron which gives excellent results. Keep your iron and board to hand so that when you make up your projects, you can "press as you sew" to give a truly professional finish.

Working from a chart

Working a cross-stitch design from a colour chart is relatively easy. Each square on the chart represents one cross-stitch worked over a particular number of fabric threads; the exact number is given with each project.

Always begin your embroidery by marking the centre of the fabric both ways with tacking stitches. You will see corresponding arrows on the chart which indicate the centre of the design. Each chart has an accompanying colour key to show matching embroidery thread colours which are identified by their numbers.

Mark the centre of the chart with a small cross and begin stitching in the middle of the fabric, using the centre lines on the fabric and chart as reference points for accurately counting the fabric threads and squares to centre your design.

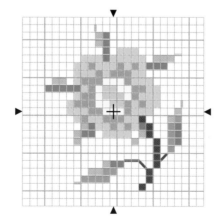

Alphabets

Simple and elegant, or flamboyant and bold, alphabets have always been a popular subject for cross-stitch embroidery. The styles may vary enormously from the single line example used in the sampler on page 14 to the highly decorative type chosen for the bookmark on page 34.

Following the appropriate project instructions, use the relevant alphabets given on pages 45–48 to substitute your chosen name or initial, first drawing it on graph paper or in the space provided on the chart.

You may find it helpful to work from the alphabet charts if you have them enlarged so that the individual squares can be seen more clearly. Most photocopying services will do this for a minimum charge.

Preparing your fabric

Begin by steam pressing the fabric to remove all creases. Should any remain, try to avoid those areas since it would be extremely difficult to remove them once the embroidery is worked.

Many evenweave fabrics, and linen in particular, fray easily in the hand so, once you have cut out your fabric, it is a good idea to overcast the edges using tacking thread.

Working in a hoop

A hoop consists of two rings, usually of wood, which fit closely one inside the other. There is a screw attachment on the outer ring for adjusting the tension of the fabric and holding it firmly in place. Hoops are made in sizes varying from 4in/10cm across to large quilting hoops measuring 24in/60cm across.

Working in a hoop

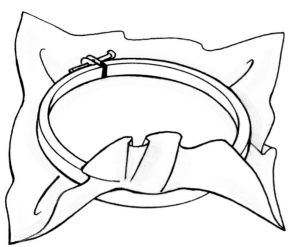

1 To stretch your fabric in a hoop, place the area to be cross-stitched over the inner ring and press the outer ring over it with the tension screw released.

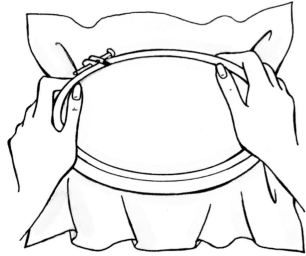

2 Keeping the grain straight, smooth the fabric evenly and tighten the screw.

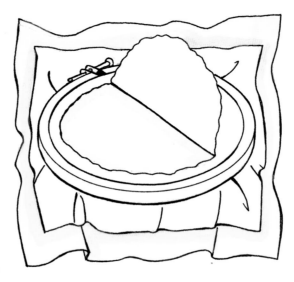

3 To prevent the outer hoop from marking the fabric or embroidery, place tissue paper between the outer ring and the embroidery. Tear away the paper to expose the fabric as shown in the diagram.

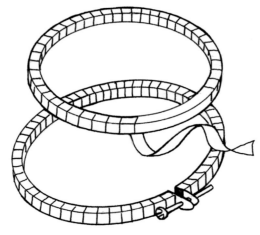

4 Alternatively, before stretching the fabric, bind both rings with bias binding.

Running stitch

Working from right to left, make small, even stitches, about ⅛in/3mm long, the same length as the spaces between. Pick up as many stitches as the needle will comfortably hold before pulling it through.

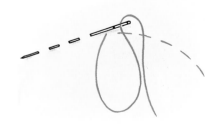

Slipstitch

This small, almost invisible stitch, formed by slipping the thread under a fold of fabric, is used to join two folded edges such as the mitred corners on the table centre (page 31), or one folded edge to a flat surface.

Working from right to left, bring the needle out through one folded edge. Slip the needle through the fold of the opposite edge for about ¼in/6mm. Bring the needle out and continue to slip the needle alternately through the two folded edges.

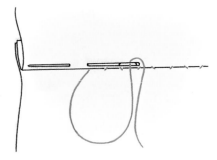

Beginning to cross-stitch

Once you have located the centre of your chart and the centre of your fabric, and with the appropriately coloured thread in your needle, insert it from the right side of the fabric a short distance away.

Bring the needle up through the centre of the fabric leaving an 3in/8cm length of thread on the surface. Continue to work the cross-stitching and, when several stitches have been completed, rethread the loose end and fasten off as follows.

starting

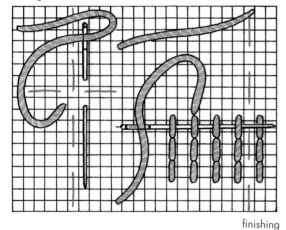

finishing

Fastening off

Take the needle through to the back, reinserting it through the same hole in the fabric. Fasten off by running the needle under the previously made stitches and trim the loose end. Subsequent threads can be started in this way. Never use knots as they create a very lumpy effect.

Backstitch

This simple line stitch, worked in continuous straight or diagonal lines, is used in cross-stitch essentially to outline a shape or to emphasize a shadow within a motif. It is also used for single line lettering, as in the sampler on page 16. The stitches are always worked over the same number of threads as the cross-stitching to lend uniformity to the finished embroidery.

Bring out the needle on the right side of the fabric and make the first stitch from left to right. Pass the needle behind the fabric and bring it out one stitch length ahead towards the left. Repeat and continue in this way to complete the stitchline.

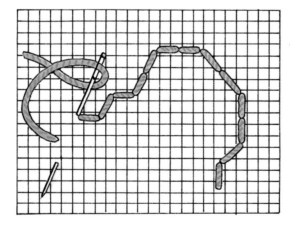

Cross-stitch

The following two methods of working are used for all cross-stitch embroidery. In both cases, neat rows of straight stitches are made on the reverse side of the fabric.

1 For stitching large solid areas, work in horizontal rows. Working from right to left, complete the first row of evenly spaced diagonal stitches over the particular number of threads given in the project instructions. Then, working from left to right, repeat the process.

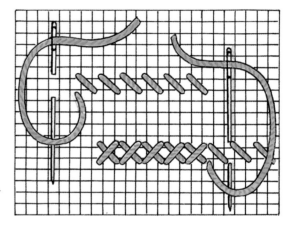

2 For stitching diagonal lines or groups of stitches, work downwards, completing each stitch before moving to the next.

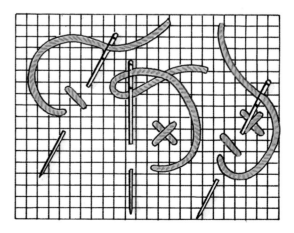

CHILD'S SHOE BAG

Finished size: 13½ x 12in/34.5 x 31cm

Make this jolly, patchwork-style drawstring shoe bag using a bold mixture of bright checks and plain-coloured fabrics to show off the central cross-stitched name panel. Substitute your choice of name using the alphabet on page 45.

YOU WILL NEED

- 11 x 9in/28 x 23cm of 27 gauge white evenweave cotton fabric
- tacking thread
- tapestry needle, size 24
- DMC stranded embroidery cotton in the following amounts and colours: one skein each of yellows 3822, 783, red 3705, greens 704, 964, 958, and blue 797
- 10 x 4in/25 x 10cm of both red and white small checked gingham and plain red cotton
- 18 x 15in/46 x 38cm of blue and white ¼in/6mm checked gingham
- 18 x 15in/46 x 38cm of bright yellow cotton
- matching sewing threads
- 2yd/1.8m of blue twisted cord, ⅛in/3mm thick

1 Add the name of your choice to the chart in the space provided, (page 12). Using a pencil and referring to the alphabet on page 45, centre the name, evenly spacing each letter.

2 Mark the centre of the fabric both lengthways and widthways with tacking stitches (see Techniques, page 7). Following the colour key and chart, in which each square represents one stitch worked over two fabric threads, begin the embroidery in the centre using two strands of thread in the needle. Working outwards from the centre, complete the cross-stitching.

3 Lightly steam press the embroidery on the wrong side. Trim the edges to measure 9 x 7½in/23 x 19cm. With the embroidery right side up, place the two red side borders on top, with right sides facing and raw edges matching. Pin, tack and stitch, taking ½in/12mm seams. Press the seams open.

4 Cut a piece of blue and white checked gingham, 13 x 4in/33 x 10cm, for the bottom border and apply it in the same way.

5 Using the front section as a template, cut out the back section from blue and white gingham. From the yellow fabric, cut two pieces measuring 15 x 9in/38 x 23cm. With right sides together, stitch a yellow border to the top of both front and back sections.

6 Using three strands of green 958 in the needle, work open buttonhole stitch around the embroidered panel, neatly starting and finishing inside the seam on the wrong side. Follow the above diagram for positioning your needle, bringing it out through the seam with the thread below.

7 With right sides together, pin, tack and machine stitch around the sides and bottom of the bag, starting and finishing ¼in/6mm above the top seam.

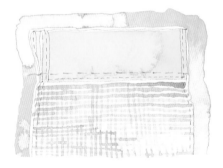

8 On the yellow fabric, make narrow double turnings on the short side edges and stitch, then stitch single narrow turnings on the long edges. Fold each piece to the wrong side so that the yellow border measures 3in/8cm from the front. Tack across.

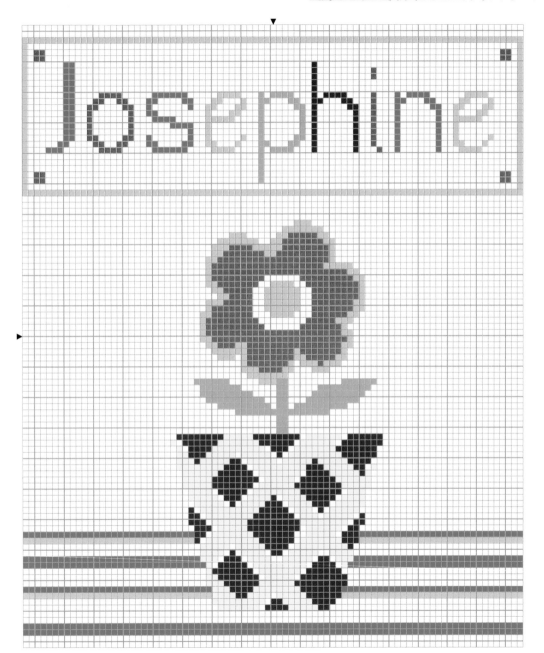

☐	**5200**
☐	**3822**
☐	**783**
☐	**3705**
☐	**704**
☐	**964**
☐	**958**
☐	**797**

9 Turn the bag through to the right side and machine stitch a ¾in/2cm wide drawstring channel, positioning it 2in/5cm from the top.

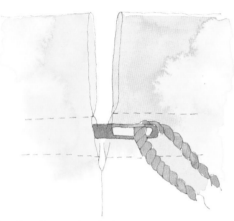

10 Cut the cord in half and, using a ribbon threader or a large safety pin, thread each piece through the channel starting and finishing at opposite sides. Knot the ends to secure.

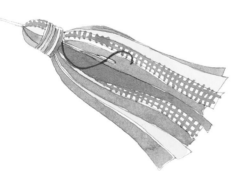

11 From the remaining fabric, cut several ½in/12mm wide strips, about 6in/15cm long. Place them on top of each other, hand stitch them securely in the middle and fold in half. Bind the thread through the head of the tassel, then pass the needle upwards bringing it out at the top. Stitch neatly to each corner of the bag, oversewing on the inside seam.

13

TRADITIONAL HOUSE SAMPLER

Finished size (unframed): 10 x 8in/25 x 20cm

Inspired by the traditional samplers of the nineteenth century featuring country scenes and framed mottoes, this prettily bordered "house" sampler would make the perfect gift to celebrate moving to a new home.

YOU WILL NEED

- 15 x 13in/38 x 33cm of 28 gauge off-white linen
- tacking thread
- tapestry needle, size 26
- embroidery frame (optional)
- DMC stranded embroidery cotton in the following amounts and colours: one skein each of white, greens 3364, 905, 501, 3809, blue 775, yellows 745, 3820, and reds 3712, 350
- 10 x 8in/25 x 20cm of medium-weight mounting board
- spray glue
- 10 x 8in/25 x 20cm of lightweight wadding
- masking tape for securing the mounted embroidery
- picture frame of your choice

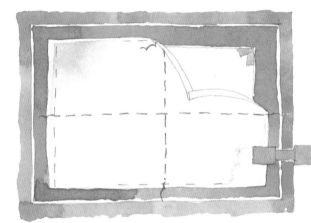

1 Mark the centre of the linen both ways with tacking stitches (see Techniques, page 7) and, if preferred, stretch the fabric in either a slate frame, following the manufacturer's instructions, or staple it to a canvas stretcher or old picture frame. Make a single turning around the fabric. Staple each side to the frame, working outwards from the middle, attaching opposite sides alternately.

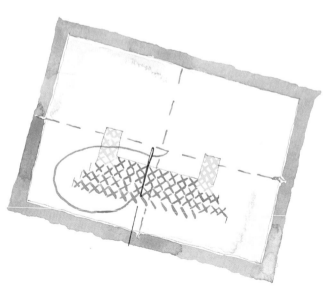

2 Following the colour key and chart opposite, in which each square represents one stitch worked over two threads of the fabric, begin the cross-stitching in the middle using two strands of thread in the needle. Working outwards from the centre, complete the cross-stitching up to the border.

5200
745
3820
3712
350
775
3809
3364
905
501

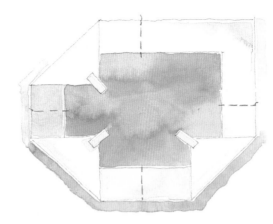

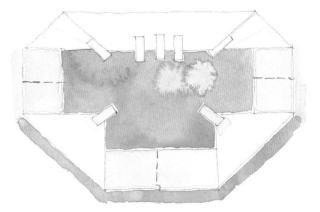

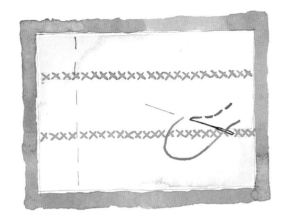

3 Using three strands of thread in the needle, cross-stitch the border lines and the horizon line; backstitch (see Techniques, page 9) the curved flower stems in the outer border. Complete the remaining cross-stitching. Remove the finished embroidery from the frame but retain the tacking stitches: they will be useful in centring the embroidery on the mounting board.

5 To stretch the fabric over the mounting board, place the embroidery right side down on a clean surface. Mark the centre both ways on the back of the mounting board and position it on top, aligning the centre marks with the tacking threads. Fold over the fabric at each corner and secure well with small pieces of masking tape.

6 Working first on one side and then on the opposite side, fold over the fabric on all four sides and secure with masking tape. Check periodically to see that the design is centred – if not, adjust the masking tape. Secure the mitred corners with tape or slipstitch them (see Techniques, page 8), if necessary. Frame the sampler following the manufacturer's instructions.

4 Coat one side of the mounting board with spray glue and press the wadding in place. Trim the edges of the wadding if necessary.

PRETTY PINCUSHION

Finished size: 5in x 5in/13cm x 13cm

Essential for all needlecrafters – a pincushion big enough to hold plenty of pins ready for use! Stitched with a simple border design, repeated on all four sides, the pincushion is eminently suitable for beginners to cross-stitch.

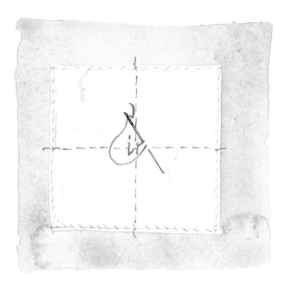

YOU WILL NEED

- 8in/20cm square of 28 gauge antique white linen
- tacking thread
- tapestry needle, size 26
- embroidery hoop (optional)
- DMC stranded embroidery cotton in the following amounts and colours: one skein each of pink 3805, blues 828, 792, and greens 958, 561
- 6in/15cm square of contrast backing fabric
- matching sewing threads
- loose synthetic wadding
- 24in/60cm of contrast bias binding, 1in/2.5cm wide

1 Mark the centre of the linen both ways with tacking stitches (see Techniques, page 7). Following the colour key and chart, in which each square represents one stitch worked over two fabric threads, begin the embroidery in the centre. Work the outline of "Pins" in backstitch (see Techniques, page 9) and use two strands of thread in the needle throughout.

2 Working outwards from the centre, embroider the border lines in backstitch too, and then complete the cross-stitching. Outline the corner diamonds with backstitch. Lightly steam press on the wrong side and remove the tacking stitches.

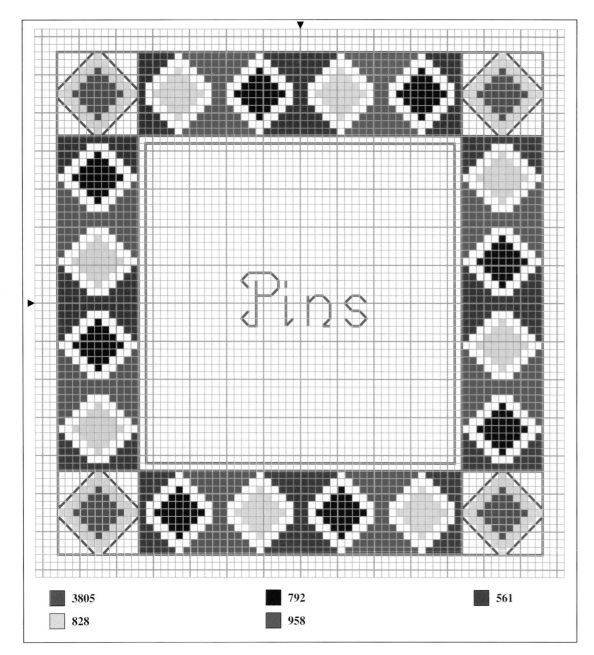

■	3805	■	792	■	561
■	828	■	958		

3 Trim the edges to within ¾in/2cm of the embroidery. Place the backing and the embroidery together, wrong sides facing and pin to hold. Machine stitch around the edges, taking a ⅜in/1cm seam and leaving a 2½in/6cm opening in one side, as shown.

4 Lightly stuff with well-teased wadding, using the blunt end of a knitting needle to push it into the far corners. Mould it into a smooth shape with your hands. Pin the opening together and machine stitch to close.

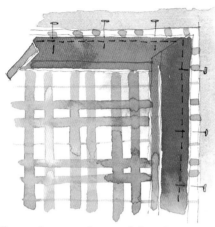

5 Cover the raw edges with bias binding. With right sides together and working from the back, fold over a diagonally cut end of the binding to the right side. Pin the binding in place with raw edges even, folding the binding diagonally at the corners. Overlap the two ends by ¾in/2cm and machine stitch around the edges.

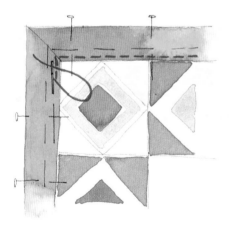

6 Turn over the binding to the right side; pin and tack. Using two strands of blue 792, stitch the binding in place with evenly spaced running stitches, ⅛in/3mm apart.

XXXXXXXXXXXXXXXXXXXXXXXXXXXXX

SCISSORS DOLLY

Finished size: 3½in/9cm high

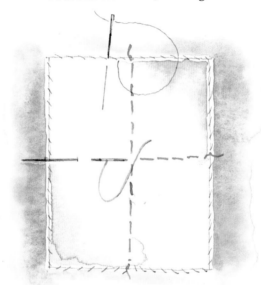

How many times do we lose our embroidery scissors? Simply because they are small, they can easily get lost in a workbag or on a busy worktable. But, with a pretty, eyecatching dolly attached, you need never lose them again!

YOU WILL NEED

- 6 x 4in/15 x 10cm of 26 gauge white evenweave cotton
- tacking thread
- tapestry needle, size 26
- DMC stranded embroidery cotton in the following amounts and colours: one skein each of yellow 3820, orange 971, pinks 948, 604, red 816, blues 800, 799, and green 907
- embroidery hoop (optional)
- 5 x 3½in/13 x 9cm of blue and white gingham
- 36in/90cm of blue ribbon, ⅛in/3mm wide
- matching sewing thread
- loose synthetic wadding

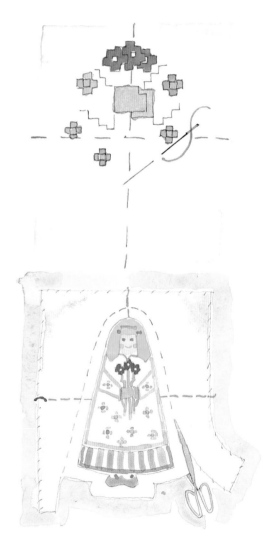

1 Overcast the raw edges of the evenweave fabric to prevent them fraying. Then tack the centre both lengthways and widthways.

2 Following the colour key and chart, in which each square represents one cross-stitch worked over two fabric threads, begin in the centre using two strands of thread.

3 Complete the cross-stitching and then the backstitching (see Techniques, page 9). Lightly steam press on the wrong side. Cut out the embroidery, adding a ⅜in/1cm seam allowance all round. Using this as a template, cut out the gingham backing fabric.

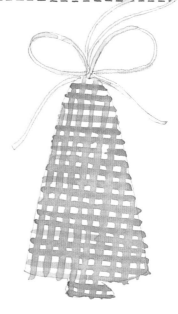

4 From the narrow ribbon, cut off 30in/76cm and fold in half. Pin and tack the cut ends inside the seam allowance at the centre top of the front piece. Pin and tack the front and back pieces together, right sides facing. Machine stitch around the edges close to the embroidery, leaving an opening in the side as shown.

☐	948	■	971
■	604	■	907
■	816	☐	800
☐	3820	■	799

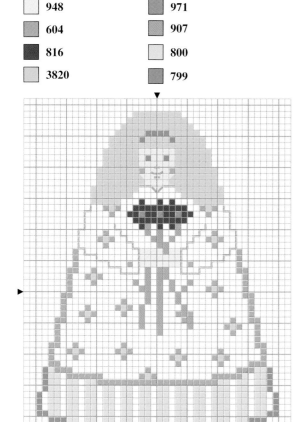

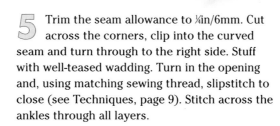

6 Tie the remaining length of ribbon into a bow and, working from the back of the head, attach it to the top of the head with one or two oversewing stitches.

5 Trim the seam allowance to ¼in/6mm. Cut across the corners, clip into the curved seam and turn through to the right side. Stuff with well-teased wadding. Turn in the opening and, using matching sewing thread, slipstitch to close (see Techniques, page 9). Stitch across the ankles through all layers.

21

FRUITY JAMPOT COVERS

Finished size: 6¼in/16cm in diameter

Delicious homemade jams and preserves, made at the height of summer, can be kept and eaten during the following winter months. Cross-stitch these delightful jampot covers to give your gifts of jam an extra special finishing touch.

YOU WILL NEED

- three white, lace-edged jampot covers with 18 gauge evenweave centres
- tacking thread
- tapestry needle, size 26
- DMC stranded embroidery cotton in the following amounts and colours: cherries – one skein each of pink 3733, reds 3705, 347, purple 327, greens 772, 504, 3347, brown 371; blackberries – reds 3687, 816, purple 550, deep blue 823, greens 993, 3364, 943, brown 611; plums – yellow 676, pinks 776, 3706, red 3350, greens 772, 471, 3053
- embroidery hoop (optional)
- ribbon threader
- 24in/60cm each of green, red and yellow satin ribbon, ¼in/6mm wide

1 All three covers are embroidered in the same way. Mark the centre of the evenweave fabric both lengthways and widthways with tacking stitches (see Techniques, page 9). Following the appropriate colour key and chart, in which each square represents one stitch worked over one fabric intersection, embroider the motif starting in the middle and using two strands of embroidery thread in the needle.

2 Working outwards from the centre, complete the cross-stitching and then add the backstitching (see Techniques, page 9).

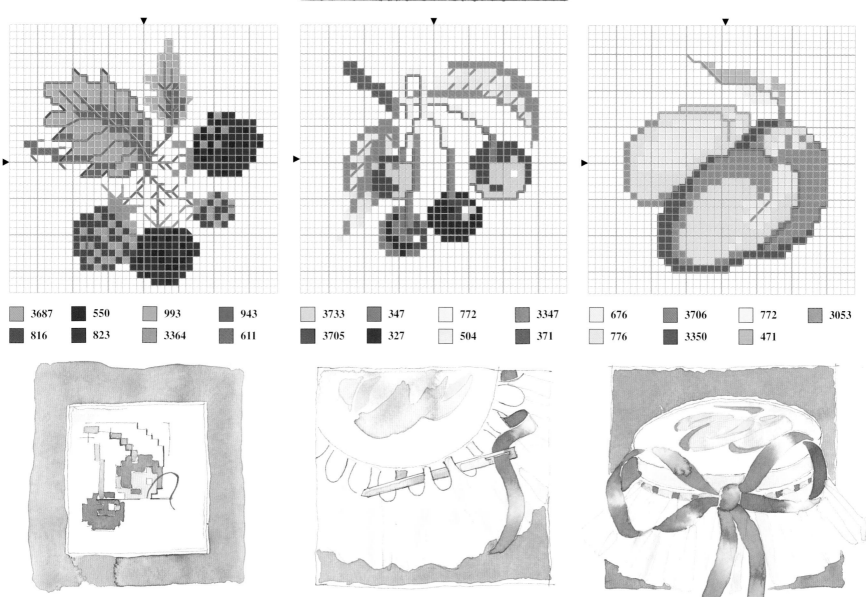

3687	550	993	943
816	823	3364	611

3733	347	772	3347
3705	327	504	371

676	3706	772	3053
776	3350	471	

3 Backstitch the outlining where appropriate to complete the embroidery. Lightly steam press on the wrong side, if necessary.

4 Using the ribbon threader, thread the ribbon through the holes in the lace edging, close to the evenweave cover.

5 Place over the jampot and tie the ribbon into a pretty bow.

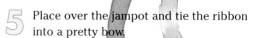

COATHANGER WITH FRAGRANT SACHET

Finished size of the coathanger, excluding the hook: 19 x 3in/48 x 8cm;
sachet: 3½ x 3in/9 x 8cm

A *padded coathanger, prettily edged with a silk frill and with a scented matching sachet, makes a welcome gift. Made from fine white linen, the hanger can be further personalized by adding the recipient's name or initials in cross-stitch.*

YOU WILL NEED

- standard wooden coathanger
- sheet of paper, size A3
- two pieces 21 x 6in/53 x 15cm of off-white 32 gauge linen
- 9 x 4½in/23 x 11.5cm of off-white 32 gauge linen
- tacking thread
- tapestry needle, size 26
- air-vanishing marker
- DMC stranded embroidery cotton: one skein pinks 3716, 962, lavender 341, 340, green 3817
- graph paper
  heavyweight synthetic wadding
- matching sewing thread
- 18in/46cm square of pale pink silk fabric
- lavender
- 18in/46cm of pink ribbon, ¼in/6mm wide
- 40in/1m of pink ribbon, ⅜in/1cm wide

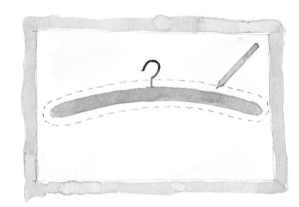

1 Place the coathanger on the paper and draw around the shape with a pencil. Add a second line ½in/12mm outside the first and cut out the paper pattern.

2 On one of the larger pieces of linen, mark the centre both lengthways and widthways with tacking stitches. Position the paper pattern centrally on the linen and draw around it using the air-vanishing marker. Tack the outline. Fold the smaller piece of linen in half widthways and, on the front section, mark the hem 1in/2.5cm down from the top edge. In the remaining area, mark the centre both ways with tacking stitches.

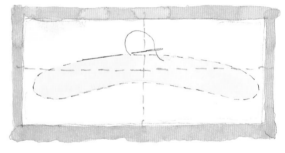

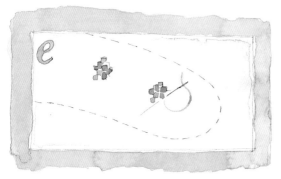

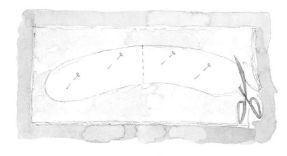

4 Following the tacked outline, cut out the embroidery, adding a ½in/12mm seam allowance all round. Now cut out the back section using the front as a template. Cut out two pieces of wadding using the paper pattern.

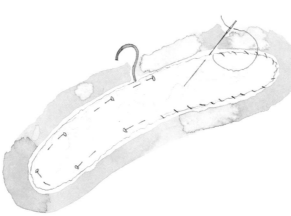

6 For the frill, cut bias strips from the silk, 2½in/6cm wide and join them together, as shown, to make one and a half times the length of the outside edge of the padded coathanger. Join to form a circle. Fold the silk in half lengthways and run a gathering thread ⅜in/1cm from the raw edges. Place on the right side of the embroidery, pull up the gathers to fit; pin, tack and machine stitch within the seam allowance.

3 Following the alphabet given on page 47, draw your chosen name on graph paper, positioning it as shown in the chart, page 26. Referring to the appropriate colour key and chart, in which each square represents one cross-stitch worked over two threads of fabric, begin the cross-stitching in the middle, using two strands of embroidery thread in the needle. Complete the embroidery on the hanger and the sachet and press on the wrong side.

5 Place the wadding on each side of the coathanger; pin and oversew the edges together.

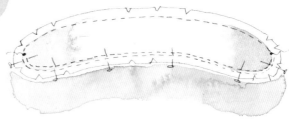

7 With right sides facing, pin, tack and stitch the front and back together, leaving the top edge open. Clip into the curved seam and turn right side out.

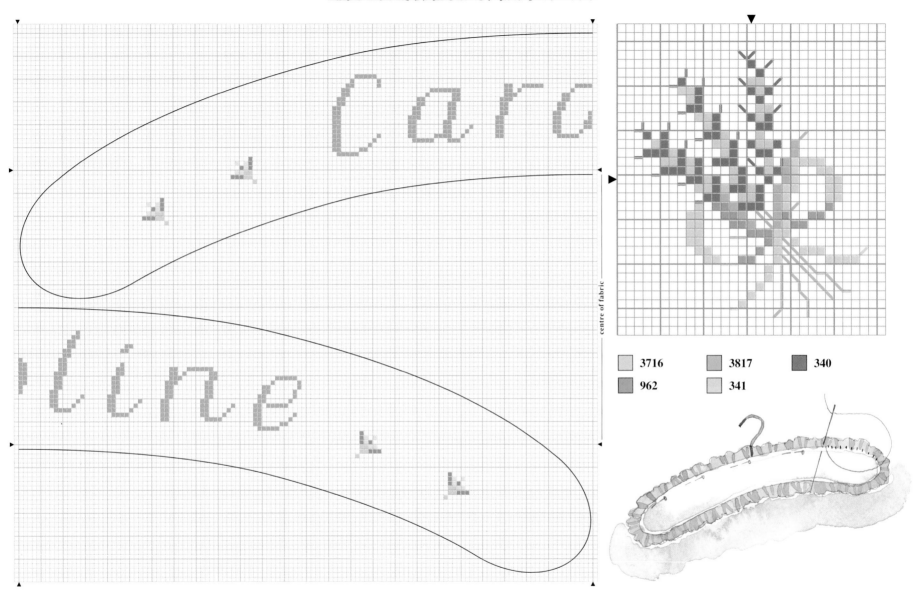

	3716		3817		340
	962		341		

centre of fabric

8 Insert the padded coathanger. Working from the back, fold in the top edges; pin and slipstitch to close the opening.

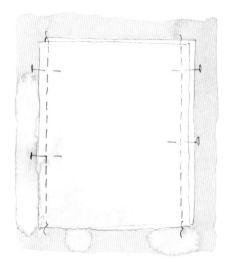

10 Make a ⅛in/12mm double turning on the top edge; pin and stitch. Cut across the corners and turn right side out. Half fill with scented lavender.

11 Gather the top, tie on the narrow ribbon and knot firmly. Knot the ends of the ribbon and slip it over the coathanger hook. Tie the remaining ribbon around the base of the hook, covering the knot of the sachet ribbon, and finish with a bow.

9 For the sachet, fold the fabric in half widthways as in step two, then pin and stitch the two sides together, leaving the top open. Press the seams open.

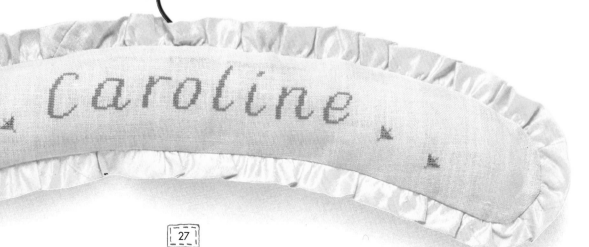

WILD FLOWER PAPERWEIGHTS

Finished size: 3¾in/9.5cm across

Colourful and delicate wild flowers make pretty motifs for glass paperweights. These single flower heads are quick and easy to work and, for economy, may be made from remnants of evenweave fabric.

YOU WILL NEED

- 36in/15cm squares of white 18 gauge Aida fabric
- tacking thread
- tapestry needle, size 26
- DMC stranded embroidery cotton in the following amounts and colours: ragwort – one skein each of yellows 3078, 744, 3820, greens 472, 989, 905; poppy – pinks 3326, 3712, reds 606, 326, greens 472, 966, black 310; mallow – pinks 819, 3689, 604, 3608, 3805, greens 504, 320
- three round glass-topped paperweights measuring 3¾in/9.5cm across

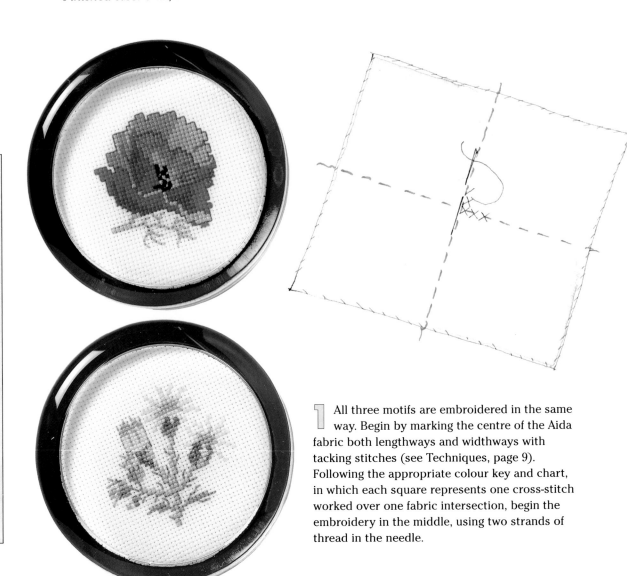

1 All three motifs are embroidered in the same way. Begin by marking the centre of the Aida fabric both lengthways and widthways with tacking stitches (see Techniques, page 9). Following the appropriate colour key and chart, in which each square represents one cross-stitch worked over one fabric intersection, begin the embroidery in the middle, using two strands of thread in the needle.

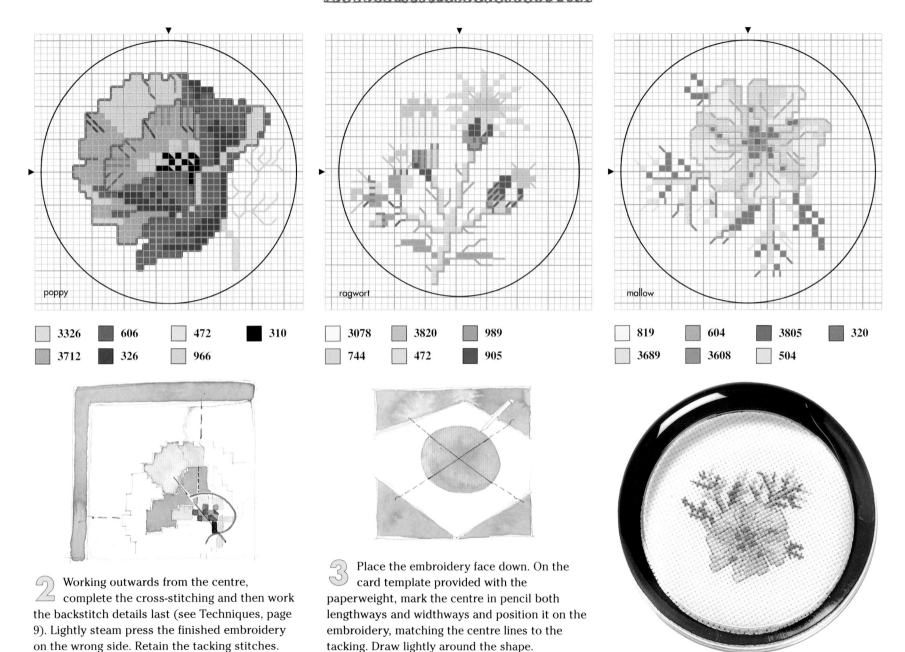

poppy

	3326		606		472		310
	3712		326		966		

ragwort

	3078		3820		989
	744		472		905

mallow

	819		604		3805		320
	3689		3608		504		

2 Working outwards from the centre, complete the cross-stitching and then work the backstitch details last (see Techniques, page 9). Lightly steam press the finished embroidery on the wrong side. Retain the tacking stitches.

3 Place the embroidery face down. On the card template provided with the paperweight, mark the centre in pencil both lengthways and widthways and position it on the embroidery, matching the centre lines to the tacking. Draw lightly around the shape.

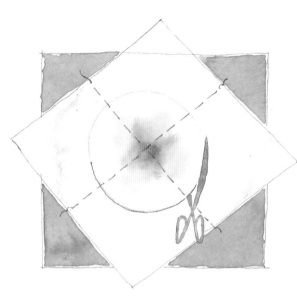

4 Make sure your embroidery is centred in the drawn circle by holding it up to the light, then cut it out. Carefully remove the remaining tacking threads.

6 Remove the backing paper from the self-adhesive felt backing (provided with the paperweight) and carefully cover the base of the paperweight. Press firmly to secure the embroidery.

5 Place the glass paperweight face down, and put the cut-out embroidery inside the indented circle where it will fit snugly.

FLORAL TABLE CENTRE

Finished size: 22½ x 15½in/57 x 39cm

A *vase of cheery summer flowers makes a pleasing design for a table centre, or it could easily double as a tray cloth. Worked on off-white linen the hem is decorated with open herringbone stitch in a variety of colours; an assortment of colours is also used for the random running stitches on the inner border.*

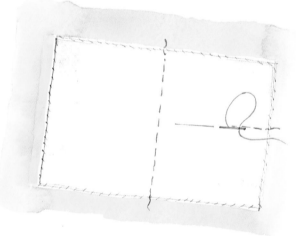

YOU WILL NEED

- 24 x 17in/60 x 42cm of off-white 25 gauge linen
- tacking thread
- tapestry needle, size 26
- DMC stranded embroidery cotton in the following amounts and colours: one skein each of yellows 445, 725, 977, 741, peaches 951, 754, pinks 605, 3731, blues 775, 799, and greens 772, 3817, 913, 3012, 501
- matching sewing thread
- crewel needle, size 5

1 Overcast the raw edges of the linen to prevent it from fraying. Then mark the centre both lengthways and widthways with tacking stitches (see Techniques, page 9).

2 Following the colour key and chart, in which each square represents one cross-stitch worked over two fabric threads, start the embroidery in the middle using two strands of thread in the needle. Work outwards from the centre, completing the cross-stitching before working the backstitch details (see Techniques, page 9). Lightly steam press the finished embroidery on the wrong side.

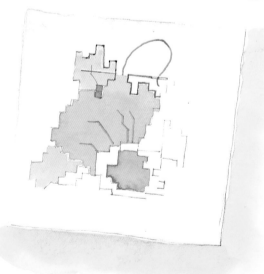

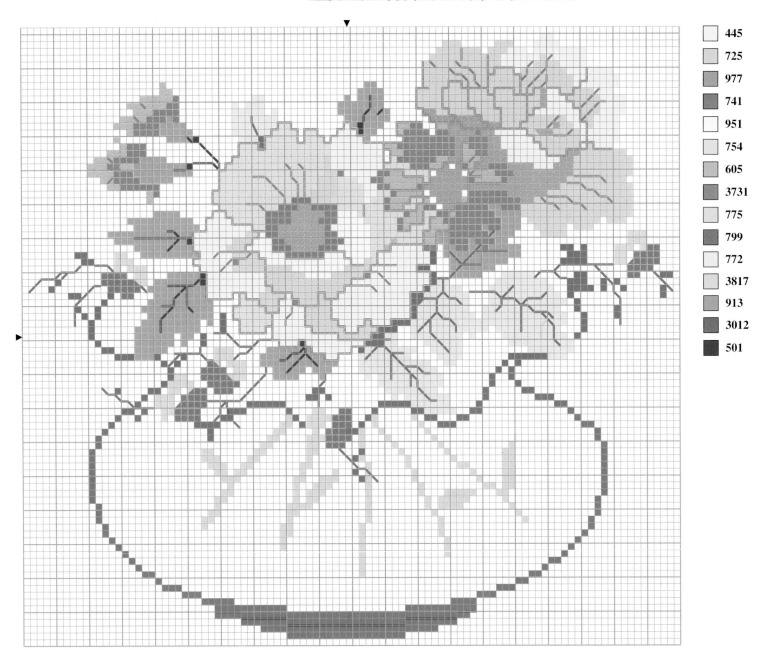

	445
	725
	977
	741
	951
	754
	605
	3731
	775
	799
	772
	3817
	913
	3012
	501

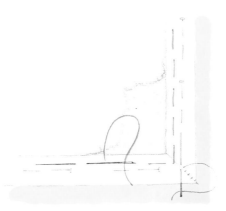

3 Trim the fabric so that it measures 25½ x 18½in/65 x 47cm, using the tacking stitches as a guide to cut all sides evenly. With wrong sides facing, make ⅜in/1cm double turnings on all sides and press the folds. Fold over the corners and trim across, as shown.

5 Using blues and greens at random and two strands of thread in the crewel needle, work herringbone stitch around the hem on the right side, holding down the hem at the same time. Working from left to right, make a small stitch through single fabric. Pull out the needle and, with the thread above, make a similar stitch below and to the right, through two layers of the hem only. Repeat the sequence to complete the hem.

6 Work the 1¼in/3cm wide inner border in running stitches placed 1in/2.5cm inside the hem. Fill this with random straight stitches using the paler pinks and yellows.

4 Refold the hem, mitring the corners, pin and tack to hold. Using matching thread, secure the mitred corners with slipstitch (see Techniques, page 9).

INITIALLED BOOKMARK

Finished size, including the tassel: 10 x 2in/25 x 5cm

This easy-to-make bookmark is worked in just one colour on prepared evenweave band, prettily finished with a looped edging. Cross-stitch the background for your chosen initial (see page 48) in any colour, and finish the pointed end with a handmade tassel.

YOU WILL NEED

- 9in/23cm of 15 gauge white evenweave band, 2in/5cm wide
- tacking thread
- tapestry needle, size 24
- DMC stranded embroidery cotton: one skein of blue 3766
- matching sewing thread
- medium-sized sewing needle

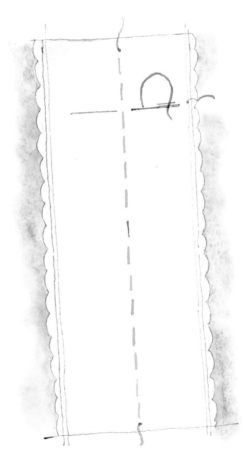

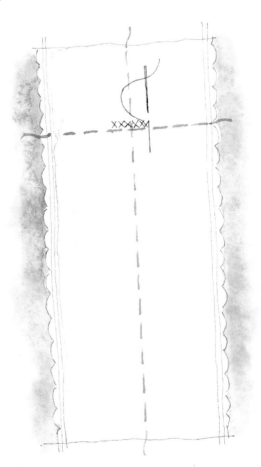

1 Mark the vertical centre of the evenweave band with tacking stitches and, following the positioning lines on the chart opposite, mark the centre of the initial 21 threads in from the top raw edge.

2 Following the colour key and chart in which each square represents one cross-stitch worked over one thread intersection, use two strands of thread in the needle to work the embroidery, starting from the centre.

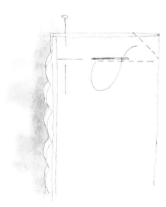

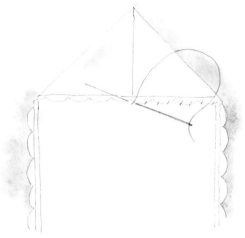

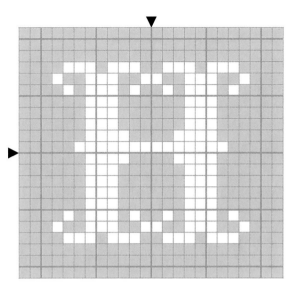

3766

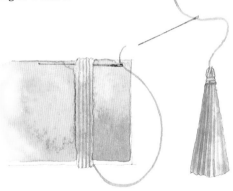

3 Lightly steam press the completed embroidery on the wrong side, if necessary. Make a small double turning on the top edge, leaving a border of two thread intersections, as shown. Using matching sewing thread, hem in place.

4 To make a point at the opposite end, fold the bookmark in half lengthways, right sides together. Use backstitch to join the short edges, taking a ⅜in/1cm seam. Trim the corner, and press the seam open.

5 Turn the point through to the right side. Flatten out the bookmark, creating a neat point. Press on the wrong side and slipstitch the turning to secure.

6 Make the tassel by winding white tacking thread around a small piece of card, 1¼in/3cm wide. Thread the loose end into a needle, slip the tassel threads off the card and wind the loose thread several times around them, close to the top. Pass the needle up through the bound threads and bring it out at the top of the tassel ready to be sewn to the point of the bookmark. Cut through the loops to finish.

MINIATURE PRIZE PIG PICTURE

Finished unframed size: 8 x 7in/20 x 18cm

This tiny cross-stitched picture, worked on pale sky-blue linen, shows a prize pig eating flowers in a meadow, and is framed with a deep border of yellow and white gingham fabric. The grass may be quickly worked using a large cross-stitch.

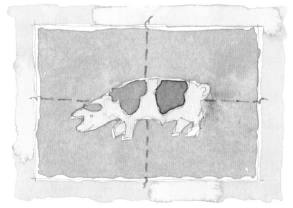

YOU WILL NEED

- 7 x 6in/18 x 15cm of 28 gauge pale blue linen
- tacking thread
- tapestry needle, size 26
- DMC stranded embroidery cotton in the following amounts and colours: one skein each of white, yellow 743, peaches 3774, 353, red 817, greens 704, 470, 501, and greys 3072, 3799
- embroidery hoop (optional)
- 16 x 9in/40.5 x 23cm of yellow and white gingham for the border
- matching sewing threads
- 8 x 7in/20 x 18cm synthetic wadding
- 8 x 7in/20 x 18cm of medium-weight mounting board
- masking tape
- picture frame of your choice

1 Mark the centre of the linen both lengthways and widthways with tacking stitches (see Techniques, page 7) and, following the colour key and chart, in which each square represents one stitch worked over two fabric threads, begin the cross-stich in the centre using two strands of embroidery thread in the needle. Complete the pig, clouds and trees.

2 Using two strands of green 704 in the needle, embroider the grass, working the cross-stitch over two fabric threads across by four fabric threads down. Fill in around the pig and flowers with half and quarter stitches. Add the backstitch details (see Techniques, page 9) and the outer border to complete the picture.

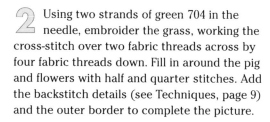

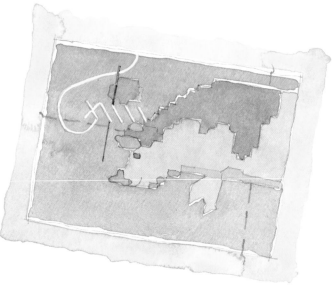

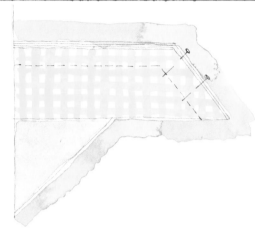

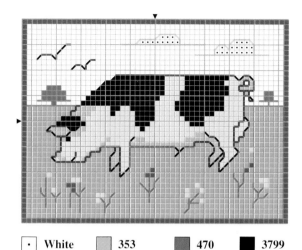

· White		353		470		3799
743		817		501		
3774		704		3072		

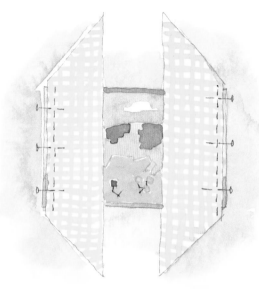

3 Lightly steam press the embroidery on the wrong side. From the gingham fabric cut two pieces 9 x 3in/23 x 8cm and two 8 x 3in/20.5 x 8cm for the border. With right sides together, pin and stitch the two shorter pieces to the short sides of the picture, taking a ½in/12mm seam.

4 Press the seams open and repeat on the two long sides, stitching to within the seam allowance at each side.

5 Working from the wrong side, place two adjacent borders together, and pin the two mitred edges to hold. Tack and stitch as shown. Repeat on each corner.

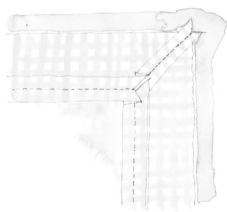

6 Remove the tacking stitches and trim the seams at the corners. Press the seam allowances open. Stretch the embroidery over mounting board with the wadding in between, securing with pieces of masking tape, ready to insert into the picture frame, following the instructions for the sampler on page 16.

GREETINGS CARDS

Finished overall size: 8 x 5½in/20 x 14cm with a cut-out measuring 5½ x 3¾in/14 x 9.5cm

YOU WILL NEED

BIRTHDAY CARD:

- 8 x 6in/20 x 15cm of pale blue 28 gauge evenweave fabric
- card mount with oval cut-out

NEW BABY CARD:

- 8 x 6in/20 x 15cm of white 18 gauge Aida fabric
- card mount with landscape cut-out
- small pearl beads
- 14in/36cm of turquoise blue satin ribbon, ¼in/6mm wide

GET WELL CARD:

- 8 x 6in/20 x 15cm of red 28 gauge evenweave fabric
- card mount with portrait cut-out
- tacking thread
- tapestry needle, size 26
- DMC stranded embroidery cotton in the following amounts and colours: birthday – one skein each of yellow 745, apricot 402, pinks 963, 3326, 962, red 3726, greens 907, 913, 905; new baby – one skein each of turquoise blue 3811, 3766, greens 472, 580, pinks 3727, 3688; get well – one skein each of yellow 743, red 917, greens 704, 993, 699, blue 792

A birthday celebration, welcoming a new baby or sending a get well message are all important occasions which we like to mark with something special. And what better way to show you care than with your own hand-embroidered card?

1 All three cards are embroidered in the same way. Overcast the raw edges of the fabric and mark the centre both lengthways and widthways with tacking stitches (see Techniques, page 9). Following the appropriate colour key and chart, in which each square represents one cross-stitch worked over two fabric threads – with the exception of the New Baby card which is over one fabric intersection – begin the embroidery in the middle using two strands of thread in the needle.

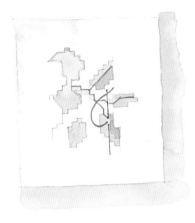

2 Complete the cross-stitching and then add the backstitch details (see Techniques, page 9). For the Birthday card, use one strand of green 905 for the leaf veins.

4 For the Get Well card, use two strands of green 699 to backstitch the message. Complete the embroidery and lightly steam press on the wrong side if necessary. Retain the tacking stitches – they will be useful for centring the design in the card mount.

6 Remove the tacking stitches, re-position the embroidery and fold over the left-hand section of the card. Press firmly. For the New Baby card, fold the ribbon in half and attach it to the inner frame, as shown, then tie it in a bow to finish.

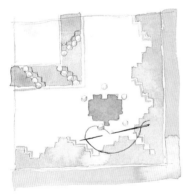

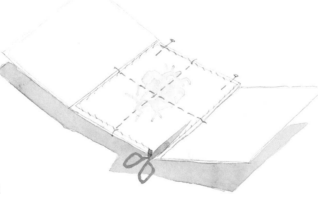

3 For the New Baby card, sew tiny pearl beads to the inner frame and around the hearts, as shown on the chart. Bring out the needle in the correct place, thread on a pearl and re-insert the needle into the same hole. Make a stitch the length of the pearl and bring it out with the thread below the needle. Take the needle through to the back, just beyond where it last emerged, and out again ready to sew on the next pearl.

5 Open out the self-adhesive card mount and place the embroidery over the cut-out area, using the tacking stitches to centre it. Trim the fabric so that it is ½in/12mm larger all round than the area marked on the card.

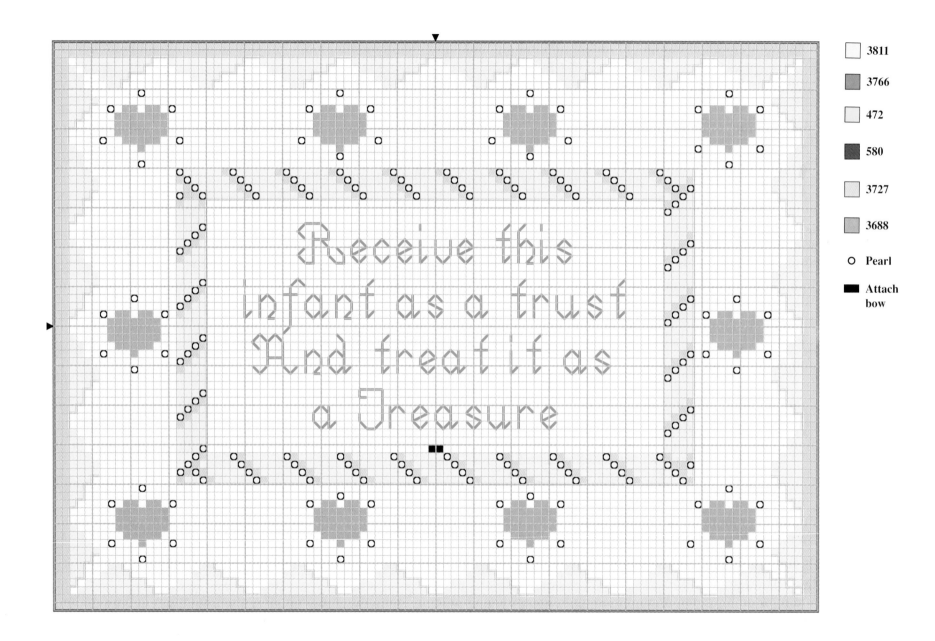

3811

3766

472

580

3727

3688

○ Pearl

■ Attach bow

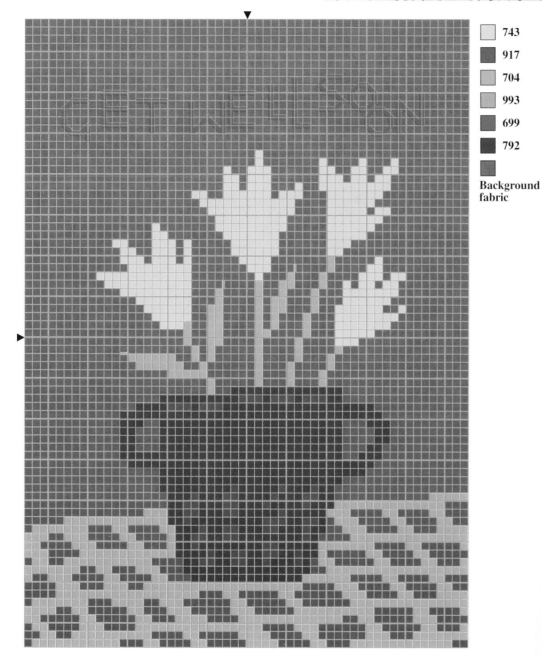

743		745	
917		402	
704		963	
993		3326	
699		962	
792		3726	
		907	
Background fabric		913	
		905	

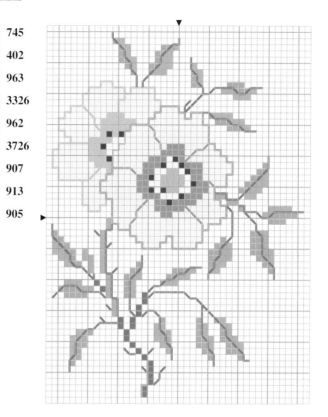

CHRISTMAS TREE DECORATIONS

Finished size of each decoration: 3½ x 3in/9 x 8cm

YOU WILL NEED

- three 6in/15cm squares of 14 gauge red Aida fabric
- tacking thread
- tapestry needle, size 24
- DMC stranded embroidery cotton: one skein each of white and red 606
- embroidery hoop (optional)
- matching sewing thread
- tracing paper
- six 4in/10cm squares of thin cardboard
- six 4in/10cm squares of lightweight wadding
- masking tape
- three 6in/15cm squares of red and white checked gingham
- fabric adhesive

SNOWFLAKE A
- 24in/60cm white twisted silky cord
- two small silver bells

SNOWFLAKE B
- 30in/76cm green satin ribbon, ⅛in/3mm wide
- six silver sequins

SNOWFLAKE C
- 24in/60cm red and green twisted silky cord
- one large red bead

In the past, the family Christmas tree was decorated with handmade toys and ornaments, and may have included sweetmeats, painted wooden toys and so on. You could start your own collection of cross-stitched decorations with these pretty white snowflakes decorated with tiny bells and sequins.

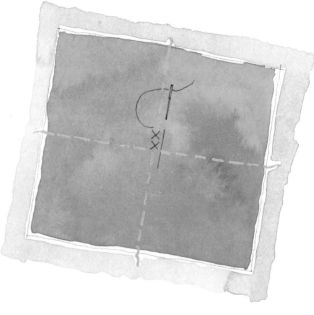

1 All three snowflakes are embroidered in the same way. Mark the centre of the Aida fabric both lengthways and widthways with tacking stitches (see Techniques, page 9). Following the appropriate chart, in which each square represents one stitch worked over one intersection of fabric, start the embroidery in the middle using two strands of white embroidery thread in the needle. Complete the cross-stitching, then add the backstitching in red (see Techniques, page 9).

2 For snowflake B, attach the sequins as indicated on the chart before making up the ornament.

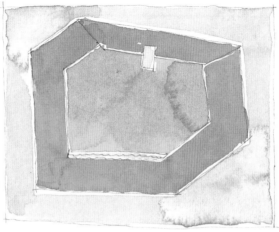

4 Cut out two layers of wadding in the same way. For the front of the ornament, assemble the three layers: place the wadding on the card with the embroidery on top, right side up. Fold the fabric to the underside and hold with pieces of masking tape. Cover the back section in the same way, with the gingham on top.

3 With tracing paper, trace around the hexagonal outline of the chart, add ¼in/6mm, and cut out the shape to use as a template. Place it on the cardboard, draw around it twice and cut out the two pieces.

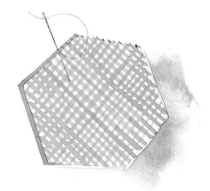

5 Place both front and back sections together and overcast the edges using matching thread.

6 For snowflake A, cover the edges with white cord, attaching it with a thin layer of fabric adhesive applied to the edge of the ornament with a thin piece of cardboard; press the cord in place and finish with a loop at the top. Tuck the loose ends just inside the seam. Attach the two bells to the bottom corners using matching sewing thread and one or two oversewing stitches.

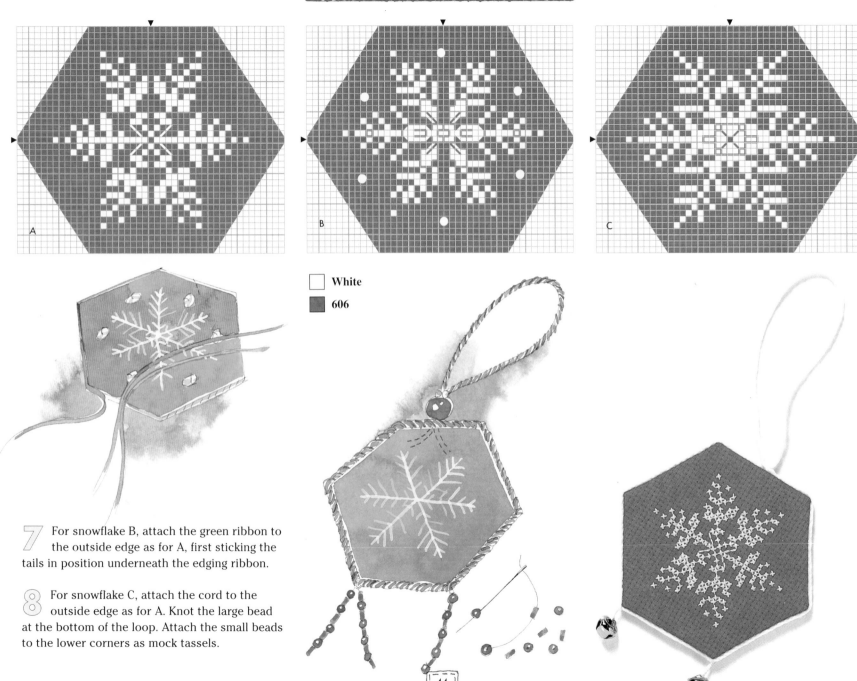

White

606

7 For snowflake B, attach the green ribbon to the outside edge as for A, first sticking the tails in position underneath the edging ribbon.

8 For snowflake C, attach the cord to the outside edge as for A. Knot the large bead at the bottom of the loop. Attach the small beads to the lower corners as mock tassels.

44

CHILD'S SHOE BAG

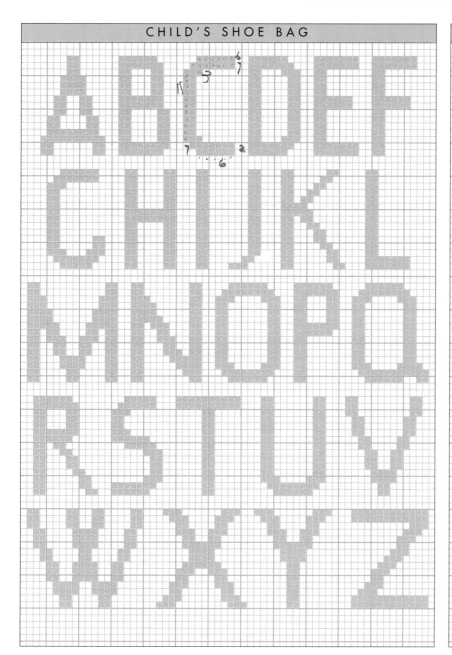

CHILD'S SHOE BAG

TRADITIONAL HOUSE SAMPLER

TRADITIONAL HOUSE SAMPLER

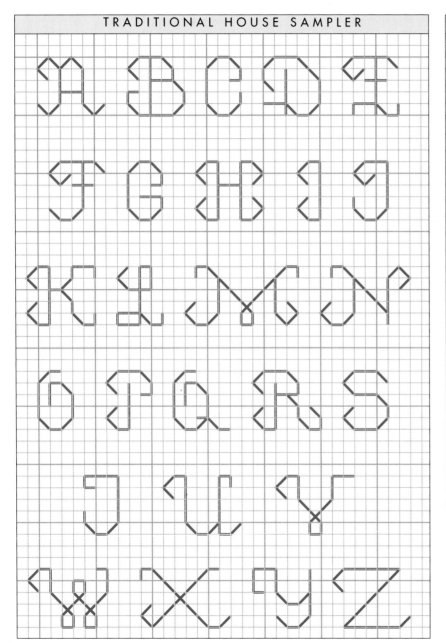

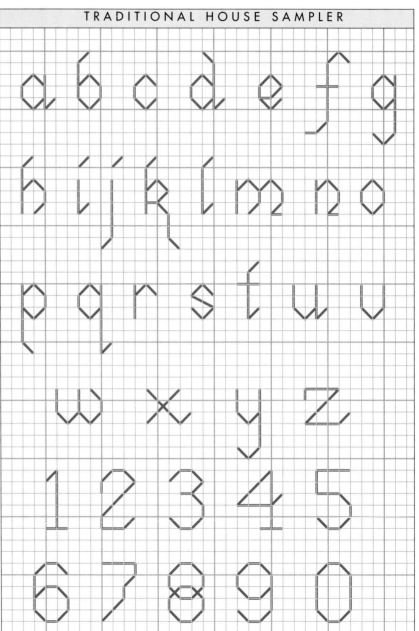

COATHANGER

COATHANGER

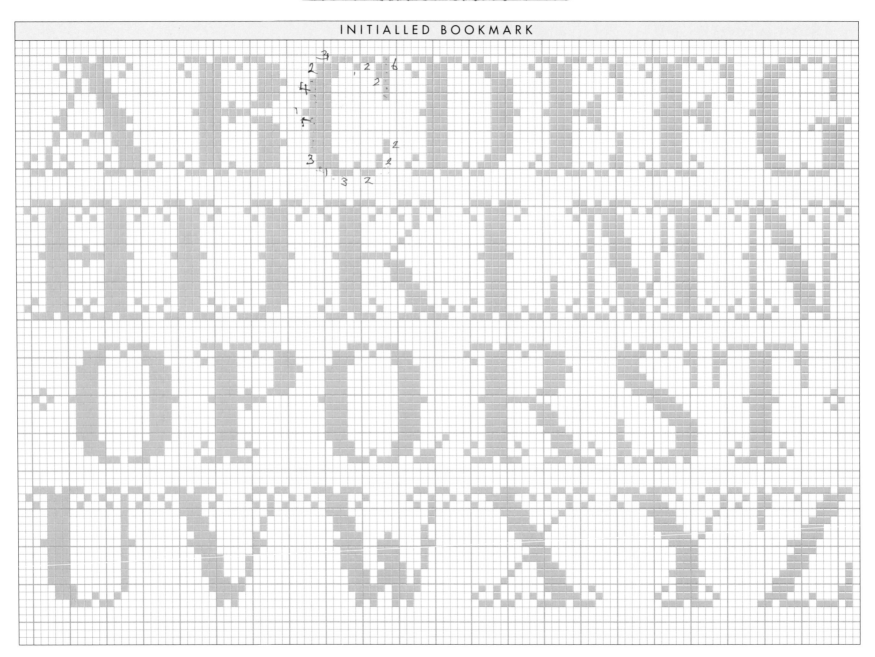

INITIALLED BOOKMARK